RE

CONTENTS

A WORD FROM THE ORIGINAL AUTHOR

I was inspired to create this book in the hopes that it would bring enjoyment to anyone who follows Canadian politics. From all political viewpoints. More seriously, I hope it will cut the tension of hyper-partisan politics that doesn't accomplish good for the majority of Canadians.

Let's all have a laugh together, then move forward on electing the most competent Canadians to enact well-reasoned policies; Not shouting binary simplified soundbites at each other.

You as the reader are encouraged to write, doodle and animate your own reasons for or against voting Trudeau in the 2019 Canadian Federal Election on October 21, 2019. Then share your work with your friends and rivals.

I did deliberate from Dec 2018 to Sep 2019 about adding additional content. However, on Sep 12, 2019 following Trudeau's absence from the National Leader's Debate (as he often has been from the House of Commons) I came to the conclusion that saying less was more.

There is an expression. "Let someone hang themselves with their own words". Or in this case rather the lack of words. Trudeau had nothing to say to Canadians on Sep 12, 2019. So, I have nothing to write about him.

However, you are free to complete the book in your own way. To think for yourself. And have fun doing it!

May freedom of thought and speech never quiver in fear of being struck down by what is expedient and fashionable.

Frank E. Williams

PS > Inspirational credit for this book goes to Michael J. Knowles' with his 2015 book, "*Reasons to Vote For Democrats*". Thank you.

25% of royalties from this book's sale
will be mandatorily donated to
The Government of Canada

What you read or hear is not important

Rather observe from a slight distance

To perceive the complete picture

Perception is everything

Even when it is not reality

Viewing too close obscures

Gazing from afar blurs

Confused?

You must skip, jump and reverse

Two lefts don't make a right

Go 53 lefts thrice

Flip left to understand

Reasons to Vote Trudeau

Reasons to Vote Trudeau

Reasons to Vote Trudeau

Reasons to Vote Trudeau

Reasons to Vote Trudeau

Reasons to Vote Trudeau

Reasons to Vote Trudeau

Reasons to Vote Trudeau

Reasons to Vote Trudeau

Reasons to Vote Trudeau

Reasons to Vote Trudeau

Reasons to Vote Trudeau

Reasons to Vote Trudeau

ABOUT THE ORIGINAL AUTHOR

Frank E. Williams has many interests, thoughts and opinions. Most of which he keeps to himself. Censorship is impossible if nothing is said, right?

On the whole he hopes you are entertained by his work. And that you chuckle and smile as you go about your day. This is his first published book.

OPERATING INSTRUCTIONS

1. Close the book.
2. With rear cover facing you →
3. Kiss the book's backside for 5+ seconds. Best when done in public.
4. Flip pages back to front. Right to left.
5. Reading time should be between 1 to 2015 seconds. Results will vary.
6. If you're confused, do whatever feels best for you.
7. If someone says you're doing it wrong, stop.
8. Apologize to them. Say, "I'm sorry. I'm like 1/16th Malaysian...ah no 1/32nd."
9. Experiences will vary and can be characterized differently.

10. **Bonus tip** – please modify this book to your heart's content! ~~Color~~ Charcoal or face paint in your favorite Trudeau quotes, facial expressions, memorable moments, characters and more! Let your imagination run wild! Cuz' it's 2019!

11. **Additional bonus tip** – please show Trudeau some love by taking a selfie or video with your beautiful creation. Post it to Twitter @JustinTrudeau....or in a yearbook for Times Magazine to discover.

12. Return to step 1 and repeat.

Post Your
Flipbook Animation
Creations
in Videos and Photos

@JustinTrudeau

#CanadaElection2019
#ReasonsToVoteTrudeau
#CdnPoli
#CanadianPoli

Include a selfie with your book as a bonus! Let's have some fun together!

71474965R00096

Made in the
USA
Middletown, DE